on the cusp of greatness

Mark Waddell is a new breed of comedy-poet-libertine for a modern generation. His fiction has been published in the UK and Philippines and his poems have appeared in *Great Poets of the 21st Century* by The Imaginary Press.

More at home in a bar than a library, Mark takes his poems to the masses with his live shows. Sometimes he is thrown off stage, sometimes people fight over his poems; some of his poems have punchlines, sometimes no punches are pulled. Once a regular performer at The Torriano, the legendary London venue known for performances by Pete Doherty, Noel Fielding, Scott McMahon and Lianne La Havas, he cut his teeth with the wildest.

Mark is also known for the street signs that keep popping up across London's Kentish Town. A passer-by named Cuthbert, with an impressive intergalactic afro hair-do, said to him one morning, 'you've made my day' – whilst staring up at a sign that read 'on the cusp of greatness'. He hopes this collection will do the same for you.

on the cusp
of greatness

poetic intoxications

&

hare-brained illustrations

by

mark waddell

eye eye capt'n john
'n' lovely ann
up the passage!

VP

Valley Press

Mc

may 16.

First published in 2016 by Valley Press
Woodend, The Crescent, Scarborough, YO11 2PW
www.valleypressuk.com

First edition, first printing (April 2016)

ISBN 978-1-908853-64-6
Cat. no. VP0081

A CIP record for this book is available from the British Library.

Printed and bound in Great Britain by
Charlesworth Press, Wakefield

Contents

for:

Penny Edwards and her lion-taming prowess

&

Peter and Yvonne Waddell, the best there is

huge APPLAUSE
also goes to:

Richard Abbott
and his
amazing magic tricks

John 'The Bear' Munro
and his
appetite for all things

Emily Talbot
and her
hybrid secret

&

the launch capability
of
Dave 'Daggers' Holman.

*'keep doing it wrong
till you like it that way'*

Willie Nelson

a fistful of assholes

she'd woken up that morning
to find
she was
the
proud owner
of a fistful of assholes.

she could not remember
where she had found them
nor could she open her hand
to have a proper look.

assholes were not attractive to her
but she knew they were there
inside her clenched fingers

she could feel them against her skin

slippery
pouting
throbbing

she estimated there to be three assholes
puckered
and alive

she was a mess now
and badly needed rid of them
knowing them to be no good

running towards the lake
she stopped
and tried to force her fingers open
but the assholes
struggled
squirmed
and started
making grunting noises
as her fist refused to budge

she took an axe left by the woodcutter
and chopped her hand off
in one neat movement
throwing it
like a twisted Excalibur
into the blue depths.

three centuries later
an expedition from The Federation
stumbled across the lake
where a fistful of assholes
rose slowly to the surface of the water.

as legend had it
whoever has the strength
to prise open the hand
would rule the world
along
with
all
the other assholes.

polka dots

how they danced before her eyes!

she was staring at herself
in the mirror
of the changing room
fighting back laughter
as the white polka dots
danced
and
zig-zagged
and
wobbled
all over
the silk.

it appeared they could not leave
the dress
so
she had
to buy it.

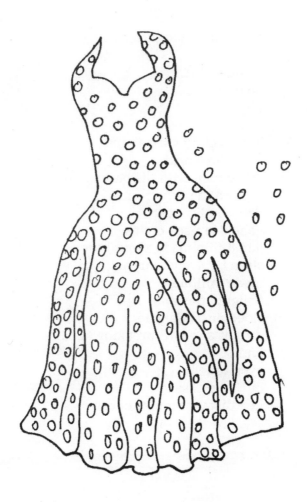

been there done that

he sure had
been there and done that
and
he never let
no one
forget it.

he'd been in special ops
seen the world
killed men with his bare hands
starred in porno films
flown helicopters
gone deep-sea diving
had a film made about him
sired twelve children
made millions
bought an island
skied an avalanche
caught a record-breaking Marlin
and
even found
buried treasure
in a distant mountain cave

but

he
never
spoke
of
love.

she lay there

she lay there
unable to move

her lips turning blue

wishing she'd never
slipped over
in the supermarket's
frozen food section
and landed trapped
amongst chicken thighs
and endless sausages
the lid slamming unkindly shut
suctioning her off
from what
had once been
a danger-free life.

she could make out
the shadows of men
passing by
and screamed
at them
to see her

but they moved on
in their intense dance
of the emasculated
hunter-gatherers.

the next day
her husband
reported her missing
and the police
retraced her steps
to find her frozen body
staring back at them
from Aisle 7
under the banner of
2 for 1 Special Offer
where a group of
disgruntled shoppers
demanded to know
where the other
corpse was?

the empty hearse

it was not natural
an empty hearse

it made no sense
heading towards the crematorium
laden with nothing
but its driver with obligatory peaked cap.

he stood watching this sight
pass by on the road to nowhere
and tipped his own hat
at the sleek black vehicle.

to his surprise
it pulled up next to him
the window came down
and
the chauffeur
asked if he was getting in?

the man felt a pain in his chest
and fell into the passenger seat
ready
for his
next journey.

THIS WAY

radiators and drains

there's two kinds of people in the world
he said
there's radiators
and
there's
drains
and
I hate to say it but
she's a fuckin' drain.

I couldn't take much more
of these insults
against my wife

but goddam it
the plumber
had
a
point.

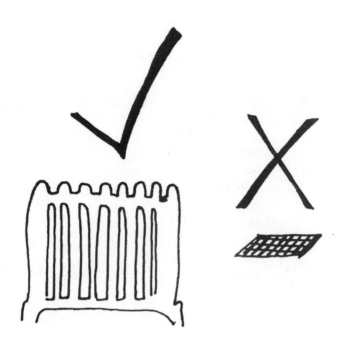

I found a human bar

I was so
happy
to have
stumbled
upon
a human bar
here on mars
that
I jumped
up and down
with
joy
whilst
hugging
the bartender
who squeezed
me back
with
all of his six
arms

putting
a
dent
in
my
celebrations.

the blizzard

the blizzard had come out of nowhere
catching the expedition by surprise.

the leader taking it upon himself
to warn the weary
to stay inside their tents.

one of the team
a japanese woman with eager eyes
and much strength in her small body
ventured outside to go to the toilet.

her ass bared to the razor-blade wind
she took a moment to wonder
why there was such beauty in this wilderness

with sight limited to a few feet
she stumbled back to the tent
where the leader scolded her
for disobeying his orders
smiling she agreed that she had taken
an unnecessary risk.

the following morning they awoke to clear blue skies
with joy in their hearts
and found frozen into the ground
the yellow word
piss.

the only way to fly

she remembered
it had seemed
like a good idea
at the time

but now
she was not so sure
strapped as she was
to a giant pair of home-made eagle wings
soaring dangerously over the canyon.

he'd laughed
when she'd told him about her dream to fly
saying
that's something kids wanna do

but secretly she'd dug her heels in.

over the years
she built her hidden masterpiece
as her dreams of flying became more intense

sometimes she flew on her back above winding rivers
hands clasped firmly behind her head
so
relaxed
it was like flying on a cloud

at other times she darted face-down through streets
inches above the ground
turning corners by tilting her head
inhaling tarmac and grime
heady exhaust fumes
and old car leather from childhood

but THIS WAS REAL
she was actually in the air
not dreaming
but going like a bat out of hell
whizzing past jagged rocks
the out-stretched arms
of scorched and twisted trees
reaching to touch her
the ground rising fast
towards a sight that none beheld

to her relief she landed perfectly

an angel
rejoining terra firma
and left her wings on a boulder
to be found years later
by a group of surprised hikers

the media picked up on the discovery
giant eagle wings fall from the sky
read headlines around the world

sitting at the kitchen table
she listened to the news on the radio
her grey hair bobbing
in tiny little shakes of laughter

'they your wings?' teased her still-cheating husband

'I wish' she replied
lost in more designs
for bigger and better wings
that one day
would take her
far away

back into that
wild blue sky.

2 columbian girls and a cake in my bed

I've no idea
how
the cake
got
there.

inside the end

the professor
was at the end
of his tether
the project's funding
under threat.

he needed RESULTS.

scratching his bald head
that used to
hold such thick hair
he wondered
where it had all
gone so
wrong?

the roll of sellotape
sitting before him
no beginning
or
end
in sight.

sharpening his nails
he continued his search

after three days
he became at one with the sellotape
and found himself shrinking
into the golden colour
deep inside the plastic land

he walked for a long time
thirsty and hungry
in a delirious state
until he bumped
into a microscopic edge of tape
that was now a hill

'eureka!' he shouted.

later he threw a party

just him
and the cat

to celebrate
how he could
at last
put the world
back together again.

it's raining diamonds on jupiter

'it's raining diamonds on jupiter'
shouted the mercenary
rubbing his hands together
with glee

the planet
being both
unpopulated
and undefended

an easy target

but
as he stood
on the celestial body's surface
sinking
into the hydrogen and helium
about to be crushed
by the most immense
pressures
imaginable
he wished
he'd thought it through more

his hands reaching up
to catch
the raining diamonds
that
zipped and sparkled and fired and burst
through his flesh
with all the ease
of
raining
diamonds.

the premature ejaculation appointment

of course
he arrived

early.

the long arm of middle age

the long arm of middle age
reached
through the open window
of
youth
grabbing
the startled man
by his
low-hanging
bollocks.

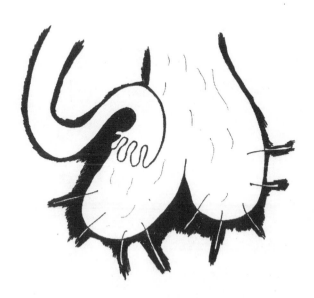

I've gone completely blank

get on a train

it was a great idea
take a train
any train
destination: *unknown*.

the japanese countryside passed in a blur
of lush paddy-fields
and endless skies

the seats were wooden
hand-crafted
from a time long ago
when such skill was honoured.

the guard enquired as to where he was going
this being a quiet route
and the fact that he was bored and lonely

'I don't know' replied the man
and handed over his ticket

the guard laughing
and then crying with joy.

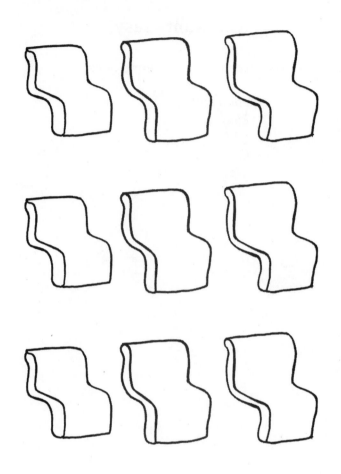

who wants easy?

sure hope someone does

been called
Easy
all
my
life.

pringles and dirty sex

the more Pringles
she ate
the dirtier
the
sex
she demanded
so
I lavished
her
with
bouquets
of
the salty snacks

until
we
committed
an act
of such
unspeakable
filth

that
these days
I feel sick
just
looking
at
a
Pringle.

phoenix rising

my apartment went up in flames

all my
writing
extinguished
in a moment

that later
inspired

the burning chronicles
my very own best-selling novel
about a writer
whose apartment went up in flames
and inspired
his very own best-selling novel.

following suit
and caught up in a whirlwind
of hope
writers throughout the land
set their tiny apartments
alight
dreaming of mirrored success

whole cities burned
that terrible night
as clouds of words
shone like fireflies
in the dark sky.

red velvet dress

I'd ripped it
off
her
in such a rush

that the next morning
koko
didn't recognise
her red
velvet dress
hanging
from the chandelier.

walking home
shivering
in
her
underwear
she blamed me

as

I

nestled
up to her scent
in
the
warmth.

a ferris wheel that never turns

oh what agony
to be
a ferris wheel
that
never
turns

just stands there
rusting
in the radioactive
fallout
zone
that
is Chernobyl

its huge being
stuck in a time
when the reactors
were torn to shreds
on 26th April 1986
sharing a birthday
with Jet Li
chinese martial arts expert and action movie star

but even he
could have done nothing
to prevent
the fallout
as trees blackened
and forests turned
to ashes
fish drowned
and birds fell
from an angry sky

in a world
that had
stopped
turning.

that's not my suitcase

I hear myself saying
'that's not my suitcase'
over
and
over
again

but the customs official
the one who never smiles
just nods.

a week later
I sit in a cell.

ten years later
as I leave that prison
the warden gathers up my belongings

and

I hear myself saying
'that's not my suitcase'
over
and
over
again.

be brilliant

'be brilliant' –

those were her
last words to me
before I walked on stage

I was nervous
of course
this being my first time
as a porn actor

but I needn't have worried
as like all men
I was
of course
brilliant.

stuffed bird in a cage

the stuffed bird in a cage
stared at me
through the bars
its beak downturned

so
I liberated it
from the pub

and
became
a symbol of hope
for
all
dead
animals
everywhere.

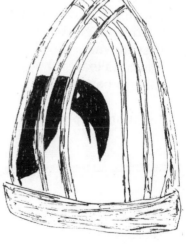

three bob marleys in the kitchen

the recently divorced
and depressed man
was surprised
to find
three bob marleys
in the kitchen
when he came down
for breakfast

they turned to him
in one
synchronised
movement
taking in
his tattered dressing gown
and
dishevelled appearance
one holding out a marijuana spliff
of such magnitude
that the man
had to take it
in both hands.

inhaling deeply

he blew smoke rings
in the shape of broken hearts
and felt himself
relaxing
for the first time
in ages
as the
three bob marleys
sang
'no woman no cry'.

crying tears in space

he watched her
crying tears in space

big balls
of the transparent gloopy stuff
suspended
just
beneath
her bloodshot eyes

zero gravity playing its tricks

the amoeba-like salty globes
quivering
as if
about to burst
but
somehow
always
hanging on

never falling

and whilst he regretted
having to break up
the relationship
he'd made his decision

she said
he could have
found a better
time
to tell her

there being
nowhere to hide
from each other

somersaulting
as the astronauts were
some 143 miles
above
earth
in a fucking tin can

but they both knew
like the tears
they couldn't

fall

head over heels
in love
again.

one minute

one minute he was
flying along
in his 1970s *starduster too* bi-plane
uncomfortable in his tight seat
sweating and cold at the same time
choking on fumes from the old spluttering engine
the noise of the propellers deafening
as his ageing body creaked
along with the battered fuselage
trying not think of his angry distant wife
waiting at their shabby home
with her incessant stare
that was driving him
crazy...

then something happened

a huge roar of wind he'd never heard before
engulfed him
and the plane was sucked
into some kinda air tunnel
and to his shock
he realised he no longer had any control over the bird

it was guiding him
on a path he had not planned
but he didn't give a damn
even though every protocol
he'd ever learned
screamed at him
to get back in charge.

instead
he relaxed back into his seat
and allowed the plane to fly
over countryside he'd never seen before
his blood pulsing
as he marvelled at eagles
swooping over thermal pockets

the intoxicating combination
of gasoline and fresh air
the rattle of the plane's straining suspension
and the thud thud thud of his beating heart
was

he remembered

all he'd ever dreamed of
as a child
and he let out a whoop of pure unadulterated joy
as he saw
the most beautiful land stretched below
with a large house
and a woman
beckoning him down.

throwing caution to the wind
he found he was able to turn the plane around
and land on a narrow dirt track
with all the skill
of a master craftsman.

taxiing up to the waving woman
there was something familiar about her

she was his lovely wife
and that fine house
was their home!

'you look surprised, did something happen?'
she asked as his jaw dropped
and he nodded skywards

'yes,' he stumbled, 'I was caught up in...'

'you don't need to explain, it's simple,'
laughed his wife
who understood such things

'you were caught up in something rare,
you were lucky'

at which he let out a sharp cry
and rushed towards her gentle eyes
and warm embrace.

together they stood there
admiring the gleaming silver machine
and
each
other

as she
gave silent thanks
for *the slipstream of enthusiasm*

ecstatic
to have her boy
back.

the death of the poet

the death of the poet
was kept from his poems
for as long
as possible

but of course
eventually they found out

and

faded fast

leaving only
the imprint
of their tears
upon
sodden
pages.

after Auden,
possibly Armitage

the sound of a falling possum

the man who struggled
with spotting the obvious
had never heard
the sound of a falling possum
before
and in its own kinda way
it was
quite beautiful
before
the impact of course

he tried to resuscitate it
pumping away
at its little heart
and kissing those
funny lips
its broken body
limp in his arms

but to no
avail.

from then onwards
everything
was sad in his life
as
he couldn't
get the sound of the falling possum
out of his
mind
until

now being aware of such things

he heard
the beautiful sound again
and turned around
just in time
to catch
another falling possum

this time saving its life

the man now understanding
why the bridge
he walked under every day
was called
suicide possum bridge.

the poetry stall

I'd sat there
all week

not a man
woman
or
child
stopping to have a look
at my wares

the hand-painted sign
swinging gently in the breeze:

poems to order

as I was packing up for the day
a small dog
nuzzled my leg
and
I wrote a note:

give this dog a bone

and placed it along with a few coins
in a worn leather bag around the animal's neck
nudging it towards the butchers.

we have
been doing this together
for a long
and
very
happy
time.

on the cusp of greatness

one evening
I was standing
at the bar
and blurted out
how I was
on the cusp of greatness

everyone
raised their drinks
and shouted
me too.

acknowledgements

'a ferris wheel that never turns' came about after reading the novel *Wolves Eat Dogs* by Martin Cruz Smith with its post-Chernobyl world and the line: 'Misery to be a Ferris wheel that never moved'.

'the death of the poet' refers to W.H. Auden's poem 'In Memory of W.B. Yeats'. In Auden's poem there is a line: 'the death of the poet was kept from his poems'. Simon Armitage may have contributed the phrase 'they found out', speaking on Radio 6 Music years ago about Auden's poem. It was late and Mark had had a few ... when he awoke, this poem was scrawled by the bed. So thanks to Simon for his words, if he said them!

thanks

Many of my ideas for poems and their titles come about from listening to the amazingly unbelievable things people say without knowing it. So a huge thanks to all who sailed upon The Torriano, my local pub, where they talked such great shit. A massive thanks also to Dean Guberina, Scott McMahon, Lol Ford and Suzi Martin for putting on those crazy nights.

Other key players include: the martini-king Richard Abbott and his globe-trotting head-turning paparazzi-fooling wax-head whose genius kicked my ass to get out there, John 'The Bear' Munro and his appetite for all things whose bonhomie cracked open the cave door to this publication, Kate Orson and her laughing-yoga healing-tears world-domination, Tony Rogers and his tramp-juice-wind-in-the-willows-bongo-dog-fixation not to mention the miracle that is Archie Pelago,

Jenny Riede and her eye-catching tutu on the bus, Mr Bleach and his love of Swarfiga, Dr Phil Jackson and his extraordinary intergalactic culinary moustache, Karin Charlesworth and her diamante diving suit, Bryan Dunbar and his words of true genius, Timothy Lionel Henry English and the hazy crackin'-on-heat of Ho Chi Minh, His Magnificence Marcus English and all that he surveyed, Brigitte Daubeny and her orders from the field, Bea Scheuermann and her charity for disorganised Germans, Greg Stretch and his amp attacks, Dowie Maddocks and his big sweaty leap onto the stage, Oliver Goodfellow and his sign cultivation, Bruce Gilchrist & Jo Joelson and the cloud-busting white-witch, Doctor Guy Waddell and his herbal alchemy, Jill Knox and her long panting black-spaniel pink tongue, Pete O'Brien and his fondness for the bastard, Maartje Berkhout & Capt'n Jim Swanky-Danbury and their muscle-building beautiful boat-life, Sara Twinkledom-Domville and her enchanting chanting wedding, Stevie Kidd and his Cambodian life-saving skills, Michael Ptootch and his salubrious hair salon and art gallery extraordinaire, Tony Main-Waddell and his hilarious croc Hector, Cloud Downey and his sparkling aura of zest, Jo Dalton and his attention to detail with a broad smile and big shoulders, Pete Bown and his ever-ready-elbow-clicking-printing-magic,   Scarlett Cannon and her twelve-inch-heel healing style, Angie McCall and her deerstalking passion for 'a fistful of assholes', David Godleman and his hasty departure from the Cayman Islands, Andy MacDonald and his Sun Ra den of delights, DJ Daggers and his bingo tunes bonanzas, Petronella Carter and her shimmering Nar Nar dance, Suzy-Q Winter and her sunny face, Flo Hiatt and her candy-is-dandy intoxicated ears in the minibus as we crank the music up, Rose Small and her Oompa Loompa blue eyes, Clive Brown and his big-hearted anarchy, Dave Maffin and his endless shorts,

Dan 'The Berserker' Towler, Christina Clackette-Lovie and her dancing toes, Alfie Jackson and his country beat in the heart of the city, Ariane Sherine and her atheist banana cake, Jill and Dave Spence and their Plastic Jesus gyrating with Magnetic Mary, Joebogul Falke and his hunger for pedestrians not to mention that SAS thumb-twisting pub encounter, Penny Edwards the Queen of Cavalier and her floating feet, Emily Talbot and her wonderful way of the wabbit. And my folks, Peter & Yvonne Waddell for their cosmic brilliance.

Finally, a massive thanks to the writers R.J. Ellory, Toni Davidson and Jeremy Page, beat-poet legend Michael Horovitz and the musicians Mark Archer of Blowout Sax, Scott McMahon and Stephen Jones aka Babybird for their blind belief! And of course, thumbs up to VP's ever-beavering away Jamie McGarry, without whom this mischievous book would not be in your grubby hands.